Just another afternoon

I don't remember us ever going to look at a property on a Sunday afternoon together. We highly valued our Sunday afternoon naps. It amazes me to think that if we had stopped to get a coffee, pulled over to go to the bathroom, or made any stop for any reason on our way to Atlanta that day, this one "happenstance meeting" would not have occurred, and the life we have today would not exist. We parked in front of a house in Grant Park; a property we were considering adding to our portfolio of homes we remodeled, rented, and sold. Another couple walked out of the house as we were getting out of the car. In an effort to save time, I asked if they were planning to put in an offer on the house. If so, I didn't think we'd take the time to walk through. It turned out they weren't interested in the house. However, we began talking and learned we did the same thing in real estate. Furthermore, this couple had a mortgage company. The wife said she could help get some of our potential purchasers financed, so we exchanged cards. At that time, I didn't know this one conversation would be the start of a friendship that would completely change our lives.

I am sharing this because we are bringing thirty orphans, as a choir, from Haiti to the United States to tour and raise funds for other orphans in Haiti and Ukraine. When we tell others what we are doing, we get the same response. "What? Why?" and, "WOW! Tell us more." So this is my attempt to explain why a Jaguar-driving, successful, selfish Real Estate Broker and entrepreneur, who never wanted anything to do with kids, and certainly didn't want any children of her own, is currently driving an SUV with over 330,000 miles on it, and is a stay-at-home mom of five.

Myrna and I went to lunch the next week and hit it off right away. She had two daughters, Jeanna and Aleena. She had a brokerage firm, as well as many other projects, and was willing to help me get people financed and ready to move into our properties. We even ended up doing some grand-scale open houses in a neighborhood. I remember bands and puppet shows and food, even golf carts! We LOVED "doing lunch" to plan, and worked very well together. David and I had opened a shelter for homeless women and children in Vine City, one of the fifth most dangerous neighborhoods in the U.S. Myrna loved helping at "George's Place," named in honor of my dad, Dr. George A. Schuler. She helped with donations of anything we needed, as well as job-finding, and teaching budgeting and finance classes for the ladies. She loved the shelter and opened one herself near Augusta, Georgia.

HAITI

Soon after we met, I learned that Myrna's husband had two children in Haiti. They were sending large sums of money on a monthly basis to support them. She learned the money was not being used to care for the children; instead they were horribly mistreated. She was sick about it. Most of the stories she told me made me want to throw up. I did what any good, ignorant friend would do. I told her to stay out of it. Her husband came to the United States after his first marriage to make a better life for his family. At some point, inexplicably, the mother of the children died. No one can agree how; some stories include voodoo, some say she was sick, and some involve suspicious activities. Myrna, against my better judgement and advice, decided she was going to Haiti to get the children. I told her that was the stupidest idea I had ever heard - she didn't speak the language, they weren't her kids, she already had two kids, and if anybody was going to get them, her husband should. For some reason, he was not able to go back to Haiti. Looking back, there were many things about their lives that did not make sense.

Myrna went to Haiti. Now that I am familiar with the passport, green card, visa stuff, I can't imagine how much it cost to bring the children here. I recall hearing her say $10,000 each but am not sure. I'll never forget her sharing that they had been so neglected, she had to rent a hotel room with a shower to get them clean enough to board the plane. They were mesmerized by sinks, toilets, and showers, because they had never seen or used them. Myrna, the daughter of Haitian parents, and the wife of a Haitian man, brought a seven year old girl and an eight year old boy back home with her to call her own. She went to school with them, taught them English and was their mother. She went from two to four children out of love. What an amazing woman.

JASMINE

Over time, we learned that Myrna was pregnant. On April 13, 2000, Myrna went into labor. She and her husband were not getting along at the time, and he was not there to help her. Myrna was so distraught, she had me take her to Northside Hospital to stay by her side as this beautiful baby girl entered the world. She had not been able to come up with a name and delegated that responsibility to me. It was at this time she also asked me to be the godmother of her new daughter; a question to which I immediately responded, "ABSOLUTELY NOT!" I had NO IDEA what a godmother was, however, my thoughts were that if anything ever happened to her, and I had been named godmother, I ended up with the baby. There was no way in my mind that was happening. I told her I was sorry and we moved on. I went downstairs to the gift shop and bought a book of baby names. David said if we ever had a girl, he wanted to name her Madison. I thought it would be weird if I named a friend's baby what he wanted to name ours, so I searched for a while. Myrna's mom was Marie which was perfect for the middle name, after what seemed like several hours, I found the name Jasmine. I loved it. It sounded perfect to me, Jasmine Marie. So, now there were five.

We invited Myrna and her husband to come to church with us, but they weren't interested. Eventually, David and I began picking up the children to go with us to Sunday school, church, and out to eat. Back then, O'Charley's restaurant let kids eat free. Such a sight we were, all seven of us in his red pick-up truck. Most Sundays, church and out-to-eat with the kids was a routine. As we lived only about ten minutes away from each other, we also went to birthday parties and other events in the children's lives.

The years went by. Myrna and I both had our shelters. In addition, she was running her mortgage company and raising her family. I had our real estate business, a personal trainer, tennis lessons, and loved to entertain.

LAKE LIVING

I am big on goal setting, not only on New Year's Eve, but quarterly, monthly, even daily; short term and long term goals. David's parents lived in Charlotte, NC, so on many holidays, we would make the drive from Atlanta to see them. On our way home, we would cross the South Carolina - Georgia Border which was a bridge over Lake Hartwell, look at the beautiful water, then at each other and say, "if we lived here, we would be home now." So, in the year 2000, a "house on the lake" was on my Long Term Goals list. By 2002, it had moved to Short Term. One of the conditions David set was that we had to sell all the real estate we owned in both Atlanta and Athens before he would even consider moving. Well, at that time, we owned many properties and his stipulation made this goal seem impossible.

One of the projects we were working on in the Athens area included thirty lots in a subdivision. We were buying beautiful double-wide mobile homes which had been used as models. We put them on the lots in this neighborhood on permanent foundations with brick or stone skirting underneath them. They were gorgeous, with fireplaces and many extras; I just loved them. One day, when I was walking through one of the double-wides, I had a great idea. We should purchase a small lot on Lake Hartwell and place one of these new mobile homes on it to be our lake house until we met David's condition. The search for lots on Lake Hartwell began.

MARRIAGE

We spent the majority of our time looking at property on the lake and trying to sell the real estate. Soon, marriage problems surfaced. It seemed we were living in the same house but not agreeing on much of anything. What a surprise, that two people who lived, worked, slept, and recreated together for 24 hours a day, seven days a week, could not get along. These marriage issues had surfaced years before, and we had gone to Christian counselors. We had been given counsel that was far from wise, and which in fact, allowed the exact same problems to resurface. However, this time the issues seemed insurmountable. I cannot remember a more depressing, frustrating, devastatingly hopeless time in my life. God tells us to "work out our own salvation with fear and trembling; for it is God who works in you both to will and to do for HIS good pleasure." I had some fear and trembling during this time; much more than I ever care to admit or discuss. Had it not been for Godly, Christian friends who refused to give up on us, plus my overwhelming desire to hear, "Well done, my good and faithful servant," at the end of my life, not only would David and I no longer be married, most likely, one or both of us would no longer be here on this earth. We began intense Biblical counseling through a local church. We began the arduous, extremely difficult, not fun year and a half of learning God's plan for our marriage. If you are currently struggling in your marriage, allow me to take this moment to speak to you directly. There is not a more difficult problem to have than within marriage. If your marriage is strong, intact, and tightly woven together in your relationship with God, all other problems are much easier to tackle since you are tackling them together. As the Bible reminds us, a strong, triple-braided cord is not easily broken. If you currently have a fabulous marriage, please, stop now, praise God and thank Him. If, however, you are struggling, I have been there, and some days, still am. One thing I know is there is Someone who wants us to succeed in our marriages, and there is someone who wants us to fail. Satan knows our weak spots, and is a master at throwing fiery darts right at them. My successful survival and hope come from knowing that I have a Master who protects my weak spots as I serve and abide in HIM. If you are in a bad spot in your marriage, stop and pray now. Google a Nouthetic Biblical Counselor near you, make an appointment and go to get guidance, help, and hope. After much counseling and getting things back on track, David decided to become a Biblical counselor to help others with their marriages. He began the long process of classes, reading, and testing, and I tagged along. Now, because of where we have been, what we have done, and what we have been through, we provide free marriage counseling as part of our ministry. Counseling others, for me anyway, is a joyful, intense, sad, unbelievable part of our ministry. It is very difficult to watch marriages and families fall apart when they could have survived. Seeing God work in these situations and relationships is an amazing blessing. The life preserver is always and only Jesus.

When we are in a **MESS**,
and let the **MESS**iah touch our hearts, and take control,
He turns our **MESS**
into our **MESS**age.

We kept our realtor busy as we kept looking for a lake lot. At the same time, we found a lady who was just beginning in Real Estate and wanted to buy all of our Atlanta property. We never dreamed we would sell everything, and certainly not all to one person. It was a long process but she bought it all. The idea was, we would move to the lake and retire.

We assured our realtor, we just wanted a lake lot big enough for a double-wide mobile home. What a surprise that by February of 2003, we purchased a five-bedroom, three-bath home with a short walk to the lake. Of course, as soon as we bought the house, we tore it apart and remodeled everything; old habits die hard. Instead of one of the main walls, we lived for a month with an ugly blue tarp blowing in the wind. We got a fabulous boat with a bathroom and several jet skis. Within three months of moving to Lake Hartwell, we had bought four more houses, simply "out of habit," to renovate and rent.

THE DAY SPA

At one of the houses we previewed, the tenant asked me to come and look at her business. She had a tanning salon in downtown Lavonia. I LOVED to tan. She wanted me to buy her business. She said that her backer had reneged, and she needed funds to keep going. I explained to her I had absolutely no experience with running a tanning salon; all I knew how to do was get into the tanning bed and push the button. She assured me I wouldn't have to do a thing. She would take care of everything. I sat in her tanning salon with a yellow legal pad asking her all the questions I could think of that a good business owner should ask, added a few numbers together, made her an offer, and bought her business. That completely unplanned transaction on my agenda that day provided for some interesting dinner conversation with my husband that evening. We had decided we weren't buying any more houses when we moved to the lake, yet had bought several. However, buying a business was really, really not in the cards. I began the announcement of this news to my husband David with the statement, "We don't have to do anything. The same lady is going to run everything." I just got that look from him. Then, I added, "And, I get to tan for free!"

That was February, 2003. On Memorial Day, after a day of fun in the sun with our friends on the lake, I checked the answering machine. The salon owner left the following message, "Hi Linda. I won't be able to work at the tanning salon anymore. I'm moving to Gainesville. I'll come by next week to pick up my computer." I never saw or heard from her again. It wasn't like I could close the doors for a week or two to catch my breath because tanning is sold in monthly packages. People would be standing at the front door of the salon the next morning waiting to "get in and get their tan on," especially since we had been closed the previous two days for Memorial Day weekend. I didn't know how to turn the tanning beds on and wasn't even sure I had a key. I had to figure out everything by trial and error. I called my sister Karen who came to the rescue. We discovered a lot of junk. I hated the place; it was so trashy and the beds were old. So, I explained to my husband, we had to remodel and put all new equipment into "the business that we weren't going to have to do anything with." I got that same look again. We tore the whole place apart and remodeled everything, adding manicures and pedicures, and massages, including a water massage. We became educated tanning salon owners rather quickly and put in the very best tanning beds. As soon as we upgraded and changed our name to "Linda's Day Spa," we were bursting at the seams. It was hilarious, because the washer and dryer were in the closet in the same room with the massage table, so we had to schedule our towel washing around massages. There wasn't one inch of space we hadn't used for something. Customers were standing in lines around the block. We either had to expand or close the doors because we had more customers than equipment for them to use. We had four tanning beds, a massage bed, a water massage bed, and a manicure and pedicure station in less than 750 square feet. So, less than a year after we purchased the salon "we weren't going to have to do anything with," the one on which we spent money, time, and effort remodeling, we moved into a 4000 square foot building. And, we moved in one day. We closed the old location on Saturday night and opened in the new location Monday morning. We had the fire chief, our pastor, our Sunday school class, and our friends from Atlanta, everyone from everywhere, moving that tanning salon. We had eight tanning beds, two massage rooms, a facial room, two pedicure stations, two nail stations, and six hair stations. It was amazing, and for the small town in which we lived, it felt like Hollywood had come to Lavonia. Very importantly, we had a separate location for the washer and dryer so we could wash towels and sheets anytime.

My sister got tired of making the one hour drive each way from her house, so it became apparent we had to find someone to run the place. We found her. Hiring Christine Brothers to run the tanning salon was one of the best decisions I have ever made. We complemented each other perfectly. Once she started working, she was there until the very end. Let me just say, owning a spa is the most fun ever! I had such a blast with it, and everyone loved coming. To be able to offer friends spa packages or a massage or a facial was great! My friend Myrna enjoyed coming up for a massage. Once we moved to the lake, we were a good hour away from each other, but Myrna would sneak up now and then. And, soon after we made the move an hour north to the lake, Myrna and her family moved an hour further south to Conyers. The 2 ½ to 3 hour distance between our homes limited the time we were able to spend together, however, they did come as a family a couple of times to play on the lake. I'll never forget little three year old Jazzy hiding and falling asleep in the bathroom, and all the other kids complaining they then couldn't use it. We skied, tubed, and had a blast!

PHONE CALLS

On Friday, October 29, 2004, we received a phone call from Myrna's husband. I spoke to him briefly and also got to talk to the two older children long enough to say hello. Their dad was more anxious to speak with David. I remember that evening with distinct clarity. David and I were sitting at our sunroom table. I could only hear David's side of the conversation which was driving me crazy. David is not very emotional but I could tell the conversation was getting intense. He said, "Sure, you guys can come up. Yes, Linda and I would be happy to meet with you." Meanwhile, I was mouthing back to David, "What for? Why? What does he want to meet about?" As David is giving me "that look," I hear him schedule a meeting for Tuesday. I'm still trying to nudge myself into the conversation, "What, David? Ask him if it is important? Ask him if we should come down there? We can go down there tomorrow. Ask him!" Then I hear David say, "I'll have Linda get in touch with Myrna to confirm that Tuesday works." I'm thinking, "Get in touch with Myrna? If her husband is making arrangements for them to meet with us on Tuesday, why isn't she in on the planning?" I still want to know why we are meeting and why she isn't there. Then I hear David speaking again, "Oh my, okay, well, that's not good. Hopefully they can do something to make her feel better." Now, I'm losing it, "Make her feel better? Who is going to make her feel better? Why doesn't she feel good? What is wrong with her?" Finally, David is mouthing while still on the phone, "She is in the hospital with a migraine." Now, I've gone to get my cell phone to start calling Myrna. I hear David say, "Sure, I'll have Linda confirm with Myrna and we will see you guys up here on Tuesday." I'm on my third futile attempt to get Myrna on the phone by the time David is saying good-bye. Now I hit David with the questions. He tells me, "All he said was they haven't been going to church." I'm thinking, "They never did go to church, did they?" David continued, "They haven't made any friends who are positive influences to hang out with since we moved."

Now, in my mind, I've already moved on to, "Where is Myrna?" David finished with, "He said he knew we do marriage counseling and wanted to schedule a time for them to come up to talk to us." To which I responded, "Why? What is wrong? Why does he think they need to talk to us? Did something happen? Why is Myrna's migraine so bad that she has to be in the hospital? If she is in the hospital, why wasn't her husband there with her? I don't understand? Do you think we should go down there? Should we go tonight? Should you call him back and see if maybe we should go tonight or tomorrow?" When I finally took a breath, David responded and said I needed to get in touch with Myrna and make sure that Tuesday would work for her.

I kept calling Myrna's phone that night, but never got a response. I left one, two, maybe three messages, I can't remember. I ran every scenario I could through my mind. I hadn't seen or talked to Myrna in a while, but had gotten a few odd emails from her. I knew there were strange things going on. She had suspicions and had done some things to confirm them. I had also knew that Haitian culture allowed the men to pretty much do whatever they wanted, however they wanted, with no questions asked. I knew that because of the culture, the men think and act much differently than what I was used to, and much differently than what Myrna considered acceptable. I finally went to bed that night without a return phone call from Myrna. I don't know how long it took me to fall asleep, and am not really sure I did.

FRIDAY, OCTOBER 30, 2004

We are huge Georgia football fans. We moved to Athens as a family when I was in first grade. My daddy worked for the University of Georgia as a food scientist in the Extension Department. I have been going to Georgia football games since before I can remember. Saturday, October 30, 2004, was the day of one of the biggest rivalry games, Georgia vs. Florida. It was also the Fall Festival at church and an exceptionally beautiful day. I spent it in the sunroom, the same sunroom where we had taken the call the previous evening. David had gone early to help set up the blow-up tents and whatever else to get prepared for the kids coming that night. I promised I would join him as soon as the game was over. In the middle of the second quarter, the phone rang. It was a lady who worked in Myrna's mortgage company. She told me that Myrna's husband called her that morning, and said, "I just killed Myrna." My heart and lungs stopped, literally completely stopped. As I couldn't say a word, she continued, but I'm not sure I heard all she said. My mind was racing and thinking, but no words were coming out. Finally, I took a breath and the words that did come were, "Are you kidding me?" She said she thought the same thing; that he was kidding. When she realized he wasn't, she asked him where he was, hung up the phone, and called 911. She told the police what he shared with her, where he was, then hung up, and called him back. He said he wanted to turn himself in. I started back in with my questions, "Where are the kids?" She told me they had been taken out of the house in their pajamas at around 5:45 AM to the police station. They were released to another lady who had worked on and off with Myrna; some type of relative to the family. I told her he had called David last night, "They were going to come up here on Tuesday. I tried calling her last night." She said she knew I had been trying to reach Myrna because she heard the three or four messages I left. Then she said, "Wait, Linda …he killed Myrna's mom too." I knew her mom came down all the time and loved to shop. She also loved to cook. "Her mom?" "Yes, both of them."

I hung up in a daze, scared out of my mind. I called and called David without getting through, and finally called his friend who I knew would also be there; no answer. I called the Pastor; no answer. Finally, David's friend returned my call. I blurted out, "Myrna was just murdered. Tell David to come home now!" I do not ever remember a time in my life, before or since, that I have had the fear and anxiety I had as I waited for David to come home. David came running in the door asking, "What? What is going on?" I did my best to repeat everything I had learned in the phone call. Then I started quizzing him over and over about the phone call the night before. "What did he say last night? Why did he say they needed to come and talk to us? What did he say was going on? Did he sound like something was wrong? Was he upset?" To every question, David replied, "I told you everything he said last night." We sat in the sunroom for the rest of the evening in shock. I don't remember who won the football game or going to bed. I just remember having a million questions, and fear. For almost a year afterward, I was scared, scared at night, scared to walk into empty rooms in my house, scared when the phone rang, scared when I walked up the stairs thinking someone was behind me, scared to walk past a window, scared.

Sunday afternoon, I heard from the children. They told me Myrna's dad who lived in New York was sending someone to get them. One of them told me, "Mrs. Linda, he promised me he would never hurt her." I had that one conversation with the children Sunday afternoon, and they were in New York by Monday morning. I flew up later that week to attend the double funeral. When I arrived, the church was full, standing room only. The children were sitting on what was like a stage area, in the front of the church up on a platform sectioned off for family. The girls saw me and motioned for me to come up front. I walked to the front and re-introduced myself to Myrna's father. We first met when he traveled to Georgia for Jasmine's baptism. The girls wanted me to walk over with them to see the caskets. That was crazy. To this day, I have had many doubts because it did not look like Myrna in the casket. She was shot more times than anyone could count with an AK-47, yet had an open casket. It looked like she had been put back together with play dough. To this day, I see people out of the corner of my eye in large crowds, and think it is her. I sat on the very front row for the service. I had rented a car, so after the ceremony, I made the long trip by myself to the grave side service. It was a very emotional service. They buried Myrna and her mother on top of each other. I had never seen anything like that before, but the memory engraved in my mind is four year old Jasmine at the graveside holding a rose. She had no clue what was happening. It was heart wrenching to see the five children standing there. After the funeral, there was a reception in the church basement with more food and liquor than I had ever seen. I had never seen alcohol in a church before, not even in the basement. I sat with the children, and when the day was over, I hugged them, and went back to my hotel to fly back the next morning. Just like that, five children who lived in Georgia with their mother and father on Friday, lived in New York a week later with their newly widowed grandfather.

I went back to the spa, real estate, and my life. Before I knew it, the holidays were on us. Everyone who knew me knew the story. I shared with my spa clients and Christine the idea of providing Christmas for the children. We turned it into a community event, and sent boxes and boxes of presents to New York for Christmas.
Through the rest of 2004 and into 2005, we spoke with the children almost daily and sent school supplies, Easter baskets, Valentine's Day gifts, and birthday gifts.

BROKEN TESTS AND A MISSION TRIP

When we lived in Atlanta, I taught Sunday school with sixth grade girls. I absolutely loved this age; I loved to see how they entered the class with pig tails and tennis shoes, and transitioned into make-up and heels. The church we attended here was smaller so had sixth through eighth grade girls in one class. The first year, I did have one sixth grader. She was my favorite, Megan. We were serving under a wonderful youth group leader named Bethany who was an avid basketball player, having played all through college. She loved Jesus and had a passion for teaching youth. She was amazing, and still is. She came up with the fabulous idea for us to go to Savannah to have a basketball camp with inner city kids as a way to build relationships so we could share Jesus with them. I couldn't play basketball, but I was all in.

A couple of weeks before we were to go, I was having some health irregularities. I was pretty concerned about it; enough that I bought several home pregnancy tests. The results kept showing up positive. I automatically thought they were all broken and told David I thought he should take one to see. He just gave me that same look. After going to the doctor and verifying that we were pregnant, it still didn't seem real to me. I couldn't grasp it. Just before we left for Savannah, I went in for a test, the results of which wouldn't be back until we returned. I remember feeling very uneasy. I couldn't wait until we got back to find out, so I called a friend who worked in the doctor's office. I can remember sneaking outside around the back of the gym in which we stayed to make the call about the test results. She told me a pregnancy at my age meant they needed to check for certain issues, and it was an "at risk pregnancy." The results weren't back yet, but her suspicion was maybe a tubal pregnancy, that they may've seen something in the blood work. I had no idea what she was talking about. I kept asking questions, and by the end, was more confused than ever. I didn't even want to be pregnant. I had had a couple of weeks to wrap my mind around the whole thing, and now was getting mad, feeling like a failure. Before she hung up, she said, "Don't worry about anything. Just have a great time and we will know everything by the time you get back." Are you kidding me? We hadn't told anybody that we were pregnant. Trust me, that wasn't hard because no one would have believed us in the first place. It was well-known that I was not the "mom type;" kids were not supposed to be in our future, planned or unplanned, but I was very anxious about our baby.

When we returned, first on my agenda was a doctor's visit to learn the test results. Everything was just fine. They did an ultra sound and we got to see and hear the baby. That is an experience I will never forget. It just blows my mind how much anxiety I had for no reason.

EIGHTH GRADE GRADUATION

When I was in school, I only knew of high school and college graduations, so I was a little surprised to learn there would be an eighth grade graduation in New York that I was to attend. I bought a ticket, flew to New York, got a rental car, and stopped at a corner market to get congratulatory flowers and balloons. While inside getting the balloons, I received the perfect New York welcome - a $200 parking ticket. I pride myself on my negotiating skills, skills I obtained from my real estate career. You don't negotiate with a New York City police woman, at least not the one I dealt with in Queens Village anyway. After my unsuccessful attempt to talk her out of giving me the ticket, I drove to the address to which I had been mailing everything for over a year now.

I hadn't seen where the kids were staying when I came up for the double funeral because of the flight arrangements and confusion. I pulled to the end of Monterey Street, and the GPS said, "Your destination is on the right." In front of me was a basketball court, and their driveway was up against the fence that surrounded the court. I pulled in and the kids came running out. It was a reunion I will never forget. The house was not what I expected. I'm not sure what I expected, but whatever it was, I hadn't expected this. All five children slept in the same room in two beds, not because they had to, but because they wanted to. It made them feel safer to be together. I slept in a room downstairs. The only boy had set up a room for himself, having no desire to be around squirming loud girls during the day. I remember the homemade weights he had in his room made of a broomstick and cinder blocks. I remember him coming into the room I was in and talking for almost an hour about how me being pregnant gave him hope there might be another boy in his life. He hated being the only boy.

The graduation was quite an experience. It was in a huge auditorium. The girls thought it was hilarious that I was the only white person in the whole place. Frankly, I hadn't noticed, but after they pointed it out, I think I was really not just the only white person in the auditorium, but quite possibly the only white person in all of Queens Village. The plan was that after graduation, our new graduate would fly home with me for the summer, sort of as a reward and break to get away. And, so she did. Bethany, and Megan, who was now in 10th grade, were lifesavers for me that summer. They don't get out of school in New York until June, so by the time we came home, everyone was well into their summer routine. The first thing we did was take the new graduate out to celebrate at the restaurant of her choice, Red Lobster. Megan, and Heather, another girl from my Sunday school class, joined us. They worked very hard to befriend her. We shopped, ate out, did all the fun things you do in the summer. Bethany, and her best friend, Lauren, who I also love, took her on a week's trip to Charleston to show her the sites.

While she was off in Charleston, we had another ultrasound scheduled. David and I both went. By this time, everyone knew we were pregnant. We were four, almost five months along. We had told both of our families, our church, our friends, and all in very creative ways. To share one, I invited my mom and one of my sisters up to have brunch at Shoney's. My mom had given me a pillow several years ago that said, "My only grandchild is a cat." I wrapped the pillow in some tissue paper and put it in a gift bag. I had mom open it at the table. She just stared at me with a strange look of confusion on her face. I simply said, "Not anymore."

In the room with the doctor and ultrasound technician, it became obvious there was a problem. The doctor turned off the machine and said, "I'm not sure. Sometimes this just happens. I don't know why, but the baby is not breathing." David asked the questions after that. I don't remember anything he asked or the doctor's responses. The next thing I remember hearing was the doctor saying, "You can have a DNC or just let things happen naturally. You don't have to decide now. You can call our office later to let us know."
The doctor left the room and I got dressed. We walked out and got in the car. David had tears in his eyes. I started freaking out, "So, I have our dead baby inside of me? What does that mean, let things happen naturally?" David did not have the answers to my questions. He did not know, and he was suffering. We had finally gotten our heads wrapped around the fact that we were going to be parents. It took us a while, a long while, but we had started to accept and even love this possibility. Now our minds and hearts had to shift gears, a shift neither one of us knew how to make. All I knew was that I needed to deliver our baby as soon as was possible. By the time we got home, we were calling to make those arrangements. It was July 4th weekend. We scheduled the DNC and I went to the hospital. My new eighth grade graduate held my hand along with a lady I love named Joanne. It always amazes me the people who show up in our time of need, people you would never expect. And the people you think should be there and expect, don't. Strange, isn't it? Then, just a day later, I was sitting in a lawn chair at the end of our cul-de-sac watching the annual 4th of July fireworks show that our kind neighbor, Don Roper, provides for our neighborhood every year.
Just like that, we went from having a child we hadn't known we wanted, to accepting and wanting our child, and then, it was taken away. It seemed our plans didn't matter; there was a different one in place.

I wasn't afforded the opportunity to mourn, have downtime, or be depressed, because I had a business to run and a teenage guest for the summer, so life went on. Before we knew it, the summer was over. Everyone here was preparing to head back to school. However, because school in New York goes into the summer, they don't start until almost a month later than GA schools. Our eighth grader had flown down on a one-way ticket without a return date. We spoke with the other children on a daily basis, and every now and then, I would get to say hello to their grandfather who was not much of a talker. In an effort to plan, I questioned him on several occasions about return arrangements to get his granddaughter into high school. They were always quick conversations with children screaming in the background, and I never felt like I had his full attention, nor got a clear answer. One afternoon as we were riding around town, I received a phone call. I remember it clearly as if it were happening right now. We were driving in front of the Habitat for Humanity Thrift Store in Lavonia. It was Grandpa, "I know you have been asking me about the return arrangements. I need to let you know that she will not be able to return. There have been many problems with fights, and boys, and she will just need to stay with you." The only response I could think of was, "She only brought one suitcase with her?" "I know. I'm sorry." As she was sitting right beside me in the car, I wasn't in a position to argue with him, and also didn't know what to say. Without realizing it, I had pulled into the thrift store parking lot and parked the car. I'm assuming since my mind stopped, the car automatically did. As I hung up the phone, she looked at me and said, "When am I going back?"

That evening, I tried to explain my phone conversation to David. I didn't do a very good job. I couldn't do a very good job, because I didn't understand it myself. I don't quite know how the rest of everything happened, but somehow we got her enrolled in the local high school. In a strange turn of events, at the beginning of the summer we were pregnant and expecting a child. At the end of the summer, we were no longer expecting a child, but had a teenage daughter ready to go to high school. Talk about a transition…

She settled in rather well. She had made friends over the summer, but her heart was hard. She didn't trust anyone. She didn't like anyone. She wasn't sure of anyone. Remember, she'd spent part of her childhood neglected in Haiti. She missed her siblings, and continued to talk to them daily. She knew more about what was going on in the house in New York than Grandpa and the caregiver who were living there. She knew some things were going on with her brother, and I knew, too. I'll never forget his first year of school in New York when he called me while on the city bus. They gave them bus passes instead of having school buses, and he had missed his stop. He had been riding around New York for over an hour, having no clue what to do. The hilarity of it was that he was calling me for help and I certainly had no idea where he was or at what bus stop he needed to get off.

After that school year, she asked us if her brother could come to GA to stay for the summer. "Stay for the summer" was a phrase that didn't settle well with me anymore. Wasn't that the original plan for her? Sure enough we received another phone call from Grandpa telling us all the reasons her brother could no longer stay in his house in New York. He said both siblings had asked if the brother could come and join us until the end of that summer, and that was more than fine with him. Grandpa just wanted to make sure it was very clear that when he came to Georgia, he would no longer be welcome to return to his house in New York City.

Oh my, so here we go again. He flew into Charlotte and, as a surprise, brought their dog, Amy. I can't stand dogs. They stink, they lick your face, and they make your house stink. David's family lives in Charlotte and came to meet us at the airport, along with my mom who had driven to Charlotte with me. When we stopped to eat, we took Amy into the Olive Garden in her black cloth carrier that looked like a brief case and placed her under the table. We had four policemen in a booth beside us. Amy never made a sound; no one ever knew she was there. But, I couldn't eat my appetizer for looking across and under the table to what were about to be two new additions to my home, both of which I had no idea how to handle.

AT HOME

It took some time settling in. We had obstacles to overcome with school, logistics, driver's licenses, citizenship, and many other things as we moved toward being a family. Both children asked Jesus into their lives within weeks of being in our home, worked at our businesses, and went to church with us on a regular basis; David actually got to baptize both of them. It was hard at times to believe they had been through all they had been through; then on some days, it was very clear. All in all, they were amazing teens.

One morning, I was drying my hair, but even over the loud sound of the dryer, I could hear some horrible, loud noise. I would turn the dryer off and not hear anything, then start drying my hair again and hear the screeching noise. I did this four times. Finally, I left the dryer off to figure out what this crazy noise was, and started walking out into the house. After a couple of seconds, I realized it might be coming from the kitchen, but when I made it to the kitchen, no noise. Again, I heard it. It was coming from the garage. I cautiously opened the garage and found my husband on the floor making an awful gut-wrenching sound I had never heard. Our car was on top of him, and the wheel base, with no tire, was cutting into the top of his leg. I added to his gut-wrenching scream, yelling for both of the children to come help me. He wanted us to grab the jack that had slipped out from under the vehicle while he was changing the brakes. The two children and I were trying to lift the car off of him. We were screaming and crying and yelling until I finally had the sense to call 911. I had them on speaker phone in the commotion while David was trying to explain how to operate the jack. David and I were first responders and firemen at the time. When the 911 dispatcher put out the call and what was happening, the cavalry came. Robert Massey, the fire chief, was the first to bolt down our driveway, and so fast, I thought he was going to go straight through the garage and into the lake. There were ambulances, fire trucks, sheriff's deputies, first responders, and firemen in their own vehicles. By the time everyone arrived, David had talked our new son through operating the jack, and he had lifted the car up enough for us to slide David out. I completely expected when we pulled him out from under the car that his leg would be left under the vehicle. But instead, the three of us lifted him up, and he was sitting on a cooler in the garage when the cavalry arrived. We took him to the hospital where they said, other than a few broken blood vessels and being very bruised and tender for the next week, he was going to be just fine. That young man of ours saved my husband's life. His sister and I could hardly speak after screaming so loud.

FISH EYEBALLS

I really wanted to do something special for my two new teenagers. I decided I would try to cook something special they loved to eat when they were in Haiti. There was no delay when I asked. The immediate response was given duet, "Fish eyeballs! Fish eyeballs, oh, Mrs. Linda, when we were in Haiti we used to race down to the ocean and scoop up the fish with our t-shirts. Then we would come back up on the beach and build a fire to cook the fish. We always fought over who was going to get the best part." I chimed in, "The eyeballs?!?" I felt like throwing up. Furthermore, where was I going to get fish eyeballs? I had never seen any at Walmart or Dill's, our local grocery store. I started having second thoughts about the whole idea. Then one day, I parked around the side of the spa because the front parking area was full. When I got out of the car, I saw a sign that said, "MEXICAN TIENDA," right across the street. I had never even noticed it before. Somehow, just the sign itself looked like they would have fish eyeballs. There were piñatas dangling from the ceiling, festive Mexican music, spices hanging in bags on racks, fresh bread and desserts in bins, aisles of food I didn't recognize, but no people. I kept walking, heading toward the back of the store, and saw a lady standing behind a glass case of raw meat. She was looking at me as if I was lost and going to ask her for directions. I finally spoke up, a little overwhelmed because I felt like I had flown through a space warp to Mexico. I asked, "Do you have any fish eyeballs?" I paused, completely expecting her to say, "What? No! What kind of people do you think we are that we would sell or eat fish eyeballs?" But instead she smiled, and answered, "Yes, we do!"

I couldn't believe this store was in the middle of town, less than a football field away from my spa. I started talking to the store owner. I asked about her family and where she went to church. I realized I was not only in that store to buy fish eyeballs, but to also share Jesus with her. I made two Haitian teenagers very happy that night with an amazing Haitian dish that wouldn't stop looking at me.

About a week later, I went back to talk to the lady who had rescued me to invite her to church. She looked at me with that strange look again, like I was lost. She politely turned me down. There was a little restaurant area in front of the glass meat cases that served authentic Mexican food. I started going over a couple of days a week to eat lunch. At first, the lady would just fix my food and serve it to me, but after a few visits, she began to come out and sit with me while I ate. She seemed very guarded.

With the skin care products we sold at the spa, my up-line, Kathy, came several times a year to do make up and skin care classes for my spa clients. On her next trip from Michigan to Georgia, I thought this might be a better way to get to know the lady from the Mexican store, so I invited her to a makeup class. I learned that she LOVES make up. When she came to the party, she and Kathy hit it off right away. They became friends on Facebook and vowed to stay in touch. Isn't that funny? I worked so hard to try to be her friend, and then a stranger shows up from Michigan with a bunch of flawless make-up brushes!

I kept going to the Mexican store. I brought a Beth Moore Bible study one day and offered to do the study with her. That lasted only a couple of times. Finally, she agreed to go to church with me. She was blown away. She couldn't believe how friendly everyone was. She and her husband joined the Sunday School class David taught and became very involved. She had three children, two boys and a girl, who got plugged in to all the church activities. She asked Jesus into her heart, fully surrendered her life to the Lord, committing everything to Him. My husband actually got to baptize her. The lady at the Mexican restaurant who sold me the fish eyeballs had now become Macarena, my best friend.

CHRISTMAS 2006

The rest of 2006 flew by. As the holidays approached, we received a call from Grandpa. He felt since the two older children were here in Georgia, it only made sense that the younger three should travel here for Christmas. All I could think was the only way the other three are coming is with round-trip tickets. I had learned my lesson.

The two older kids missed their three younger sisters, and the three youngest missed the two oldest. On the surface, it sounded like such a wonderful idea, however, logistically speaking, I drove a Jaguar. We didn't even have a car that we could all fit in. So, we traded vehicles with David's sister who had a minivan. Now, this is when you know you have reached the ultimate in prioritizing, when you trade in your sports car for a minivan.

David's daughter Kendra decided to join us this Christmas with all the other children. So, merrily, merrily, merrily, merrily, life is but a dream, right? Here we are - minivan, me and six kids! Everywhere we went, people thought I was a social worker or foster mom. We did Christmas in Georgia at our home, in North Carolina with David's large family, and again in Georgia with my big family. What a merry, merry Christmas we had!

My most vivid memories that Christmas involved that minivan. Heading home after picking up the kids from the airport, Jasmine, who must have been six, looks up, sees a Hooter's billboard and yells out, "That's what I want to be when I grow up." It took all I had not to drive off the road. Then, while shopping at my favorite store, The Dollar Store, I realized all the kids were not with me. I got to the register, looked behind me, and started counting. They just laughed when I realized one was missing. I had pushed the button to lock the van doors on the key ring before everyone had an opportunity to get out of the car and had locked one of them inside. Going from zero to six children was quite the experience.

FIREWORKS

We had always had a fun New Year's Eve party at our house, usually to pray in the New Year and eat lots of food. And, we loved fireworks. Living on the lake, everyone loves to set off fireworks for any and every holiday; really they love to set them off any day of the week, holiday or not, but especially on New Year's Eve. We have two huge fireworks stores a couple of exits up over the South Carolina line. The younger three girls were very excited about picking out the fireworks so I loaded them up in the minivan to head to the store. I had Jasmine, the youngest, sitting in the cart with me while I was using my Economics degree to determine the biggest bang, literally, we could get for our bucks. We were strolling up and down looking at all the options when I heard some kind of ruckus, then saw smoke. Now I'm the one causing the ruckus, yelling and screaming for the other two girls to get out of the store. People are running everywhere out of both exits. I'm frantically pushing the cart with Jasmine in it as fast as I possibly can, then running to the car as though my life depended on it because any second, this entire fireworks store was going up in flames. We got to the minivan and everyone is accounted for. I pull off with the doors still flung open, driving as fast and as far away as I could, praying the entire time that we would all live to tell about it. I couldn't even breathe because all I could think was how in the world I was going to tell grandpa that the three kids, for whom he'd given me round-trip tickets, weren't coming home because I blew them up in a fireworks store. I drove over the interstate bridge and ended up in the parking lot of the other fireworks store. As we get out of the car, we could see smoke coming out of the first store, and police and fire trucks squealing into the parking lot.

We got ourselves back together and went inside to try again, repeating our same procedure. I have Jazzy in the cart while we go up and down the aisles putting our purchases in the buggy. All of us are now breathing normally. The other two girls stayed right by my side in this store unlike the previous store where I had allowed them to wander around to look on their own. As we headed up to the register with our full cart, two men came walking toward us. One had on a police uniform and the other was dressed in normal clothes. They walked up to us, held out an iPod, and said, "Whose is this?" Aleena immediately reached out to take it, and said, "That's mine." He responded, "I thought so. Ma'am, you'll need to come with us please." What? I thought one of the girls had dropped their iPod and these nice gentlemen were returning it for us. Why did I need to come with them? I asked, "Please, what is going on?" They pulled me aside, and said, "Your daughter pulled a string on the fireworks display at the store across the interstate and started the explosion that caught the store on fire. The manager saw her do it and she dropped her iPod when she was running out of the store."
Aleena is me. There, I said it. She is a strong-willed child. She has a mind of her own. She does now, and she did then. She did when she was born. I remember, one afternoon Myrna called me, "Linda, I might be going to jail for a federal offense." "What?" I asked. "Aleena wanted money to buy ice cream at school and I wouldn't give her any so she talked Jeanna into going with her to the neighbor's house, and stole some checks out of our neighbor's mailbox. Then, she took the checks to school and wrote out a check to the lunchroom lady for ice cream." Keep in mind, this is when she was in kindergarten.

The officer told me we needed to go back to the original fireworks store to speak to the manager to determine what type of charges would be filed, and how we were going to move forward regarding damages. You always hear people say, if looks could kill. Well, I wanted to tie Aleena to the top of the mini-van. I couldn't believe someone was going to jail for this seven year old. I was so mad, the last thing I wanted to do was to look at her, which is probably the only reason she is still alive. I grabbed Jasmine out of the cart, pushed the cart full of fireworks we had carefully chosen for a second time off to the side of the store. I got all of the girls in the car, including Aleena, though I really wanted her to walk. We drove back to the other fireworks store in complete silence. Once we parked and the girls saw the fire trucks and police cars, I started with my speech, "We are going in this store to apologize. Aleena, whatever you do, and no matter what anyone says, you very kindly tell this man how very, very sorry you are, and that you will never do it again." Aleena looked at me, and said, "What do you want me to apologize for?" "I want you to apologize for blowing up the fireworks store," I said sternly. "How did I blow up the store?" she asked. I said, "Because you pulled the string on the display." Aleena just stared at me, and then said, "No, I didn't." I replied, "Yes, you did. They saw you do it." She insisted, "I didn't pull a string." Now I'm arguing with a seven year old who holds my future criminal record in her hands, and she is refusing to apologize for blowing up a fireworks store because she is telling me she didn't do it. And, this is all taking place in a mini-van in a parking lot with policemen and firemen standing outside the van waiting for us to get out. Aleena looks up at me and says very matter-of-factly, "Jeanna pulled the string." "WHAT?" She repeated, "Jeanna pulled the string." I stretch my head around the front seat so I can see Jeanna's face, "Jeanna?" "Yes, ma'am," she answers. "Did you pull a string on the fireworks display in this store?" "Yes ma'am," she answered. I whipped back around in my seat, put my head in my hands and banged it on the steering wheel several times. Then I remembered all the police officers outside staring at me. I calmly turned around and told Jeanna, "We are going in to apologize to the man who owns this store. Do you understand?" "Yes ma'am." We both got out of the mini-van, and I took her hand. We got to the entrance, and she looked up at me and said, "Can I have a piece of gum, please?" I answered, "Not right now. Let's do this." The policeman led us back inside the still smoking store full of water puddles. He took us to the owner who was NOT happy. I introduced myself and I introduced Jeanna. Jeanna looked up at the man and said, "I'm sorry I pulled the string in your store. I didn't know what it was. I'm sorry." I added about ten more minutes of how sorry I was, how I had no idea what to do or say, and how I couldn't imagine how he felt. Finally the cop stopped me and led us back outside. He told us to wait as the owner wanted to see what we had to say before he assessed the damages and decided what to do. At last I had five seconds to call David. Before I did, I got all three girls' attention. I apologized in tears to Aleena. I made all of them hold hands, and we begged, "God, please, please, help that man feel sorry for us. God, please, don't let us go to jail. God, please, take care of this. We are scared and have no idea what to do. You are the only One who can take care of this. AMEN." As soon as we said, "Amen," my scared, sinful-self wondered, "What if I just drive off. They don't know my name. This is not my car." Then, I called David. In his always calm voice, he nonchalantly answered, "Hello." In one breath I said, "David, I think Jeanna is going to jail. She pulled a string and the whole store blew up. We are waiting on the cops to tell us if she is going to jail or not, and how much money we are going to have to pay for the damages. They said probably $25,000." To his, "What, Linda?" I said it all again, a little slower. "First of all," he said, "Jeanna is an eight year old child. She is not going to jail, and if anybody is going to jail, it's you." Just the encouragement I needed. At that moment, the police officer came back and tapped on my window. I quickly hung up with David, and of course, couldn't figure out how to roll the stupid window down so just got out of the car. Now it was pouring, so we walked back under the canopy at the front door. He told me they had assessed the damages and the owner felt like he could get everything repaired and replaced for $10,000. I swallowed because my mouth was dry as a bone. I was calculating where we could get the money. I had already planned to call my mom and borrow most of it, and was mulling over what we had in savings when the officer said, "He has decided not to press any charges." I finally came back into focus, "Could you repeat that?" "The owner has decided not to press charges. He has assessed the damage repair will be around $10,000." I said, "Okay, what do I need to do about that?" The officer said, "Because you cooperated, and came back, and had your daughter apologize, he has decided not to ask you to pay the damages." Now I'm bawling, and wanted to correct him that she wasn't my daughter, and also give myself a pat on the back for not running which I admit to considering, and I wanted to go inside and hug the owner, and then I thought, "No, what if he changes his mind." Then, I wanted to raise my hands and say, "Thank you, GOD!" The officer said, "Ma'am, you are free to go." I asked if I could go inside to thank the owner. The officer said, "Just a couple of years ago, his entire store burned down. This whole episode has him really shaken up. It is probably better if you just go on home now." I was soaking wet by the time I got back to the car. I sat in the driver's seat and cried. I was emotionally exhausted. I was grateful to God. I was so mad at Jeanna. I felt horrible for how I had treated Aleena. I still didn't have any stupid fireworks for the New Year's Eve party, and I just wanted to go home to bed. On the way home, I called David to tell him we were coming home instead of going to jail. He said, "Okay." We didn't have any fireworks that year or for quite a while after that.

THE YEAR OF 7's

After New Year's Day, it was time for the three youngest to head back to New York, time to go back to school and get life back to "normal." Grandpa was real curious to see how things went while they were here. I don't know if any of us told him about the trip to the fireworks store. Most importantly, we returned all the girls in one piece.

In spring of that year, Grandpa called to tell us he could not keep the three younger girls any longer. He was too old, they got into too much trouble, and he just couldn't do it anymore. He said he didn't know of any family that would take all three, and if he couldn't find anyone to take them, he was prepared to split them up and put them in foster care. He wanted them to finish the school year in New York and wondered if we could take the girls at the end of the school year. David told Grandpa we would discuss things and get back to him. We didn't know at the time that he was sick and would live only another nine months. Christmas had been a test to see if we could handle and love his grandchildren.

On the seventeenth day of the seventh month of the year 2007, our family living in our home grew from four to seven with children seven to seventeen. We borrowed a trailer and drove to New York, loaded up everything they had accumulated during the two and a half years at grandpa's, then went to the cemetery. We took flowers and had our own ceremony. I remember David making a commitment to Myrna to do the best he could with her children. We got back in the car and drove back to Georgia. On the way home, I had everyone review a chart I made of their food likes and dislikes. I had listed every food I could think of with each child's name so they could let me know if they liked, loved, or hated the item. By the end of the drive, we had two items that everyone loved: ketchup and watermelon.

And so our lives being parents to five children began. It hit me like a ton of bricks one day that God's purpose for us being pregnant wasn't for us to have a baby, but instead for us to have time to wrap our minds around being parents.

We started off with second, fourth, fifth, and tenth graders, and a college student. This meant, well, first of all, it meant I had to figure out where the schools were. Secondly, I was dealing with everything from girls starting their cycles to girls losing their teeth, to signing up for the SAT and college to getting the two older children their citizenship and, of course, driver's licenses.

Saying it was hard is an understatement. We had no idea what we were doing. I remembering going to the pharmacy to pick up a prescription one day when the lady behind the counter asked me one child's date of birth. When I told her I'd have to look on my phone, and then still gave her the wrong date, it took quite a while to explain.

I had two friends who gave me great advice. Ashley, who had five children herself, told me I needed to have family meetings. The other crucial advice I received came from Tracy. She taught me how to structure chores, buy alarm clocks for everyone, teach them how to do their own laundry, and how to correct my children. She told me to make a list of all the things I hated to do, and when it came time for consequences, the children could choose from one of the items on the list; that way, punishing them was not punishing me! The family meetings were, and are still, priceless. I had run numerous board meetings in my varied careers, so I run our family meetings the same way. We operate by Robert's Rules of Order. We have a secretary who takes minutes which have become invaluable. When you have a family of seven living in the same house, there are many issues, and people remember things very differently, so having decisions with signatures that everyone reads and agrees upon works very well. There are big issues that have to be resolved, including, but not limited to: towels, socks, chores, who gets to do what when, just to name a few. I still have those books and they are right up there with my Bible as what I would grab if my house was on fire. At first, when someone got upset or mad about something, or complained about how something wasn't fair, they would come running to me. My response was that we needed to wait until we could discuss it with all parties involved. Now, when they are upset about something, I hear, "I'm calling a family meeting tonight after dinner." We still have family meetings. Actually, we just had one last night. Some come to the meeting much more prepared than others. We have had full blown proposals given over proper chore division.

JOBS

Our oldest two had already been working at the spa. It was great to have them there. On December 8th 2008, I received a phone call from the bank that the balloon note on our spa was being called due. We had to pay an astronomical amount of money by the 20th of December. At a spa, the majority of business is around holidays. The sales are mostly gift certificates for Christmas, Valentine's Day, and Mother's Day! The moment I realized we would not be able to come up with the funds, I knew we had to close. Every moment we stayed open after that phone call, we would be selling gift certificates we would not be able to honor. I went into the spa the next day and had difficult conversations with the best employees in the world. I had to tell them we were closing the doors. Not only that we were closing the doors, but now, today. How ironic; we moved to that location overnight, and were now closing it overnight. We did our best to sell anything and everything to get funds to pay the bank, but couldn't seem to sell anything. We were in a horrible position because after closing the doors, there was no way to bring in another penny. It was a bad economic time for everyone, everywhere. We also had problems that year with the mobile home neighborhood we were working on. Someone in the same city brought a mobile home into another neighborhood when the Architectural Control Covenants in the neighborhood expired. The mobile home was not up to par and the residents went crazy. They complained to the county, who for lack of a better solution, passed a moratorium stating, "Any neighborhood that had more stick built homes than mobile homes could not have more mobile homes placed in the neighborhood." Even though the homes we were bringing in were nicer and appraising higher than stick built homes, we were shut down, stopped completely, at a standstill. Funny how that works, because banks don't really care what the county says or how it affects your business plan, they still want to get paid. But if you are not putting in homes, you can't sell or rent homes, therefore it is impossible to collect any funds to pay the bank. This one decision led to the demise of our real estate business. We ended up paying an auction company to auction all the properties we had left. It was depressing, embarrassing, and felt like the rug was pulled out from under us. Through all of the turmoil, it was very likely we were going to lose our home. I could not get my head around it. We had lived, just the two of us, in a five bedroom, three and a half bath house. Now we have five kids, are losing our home, and will most likely have to move into one of our rental properties. At that time, the only way to keep the children in the same schools was to move into the three-bedroom, one and a half-bath house we had about five miles away. I told God this made absolutely no sense, none. It seemed nothing we did worked. A friend of mine moved because her husband was transferred, and their home near the high school sat vacant while they tried to sell it. She called me one day and said, "Linda, our house is your house. You can stay in it as long as you need to." Her house was huge; it would work perfectly for us. I asked her how much she would need monthly. She told me not to worry about it. She said if you can pay something fine, if not, that is fine, too. She told me where the key was. I walked through the house and prayed and cried. I thought through who could stay where, whose bedroom would be whose, where we would put our furniture. I cried more and prayed more. I thanked God for the house and my friend, and told Him I was more than grateful, and if this is where we had to be, I was fine with it. Maybe He wanted us closer to the high school. It would certainly save gas money since, at this point, we still had three more to attend. It was actually so close, they could walk to school. I could not think through what in the world the plan was, but when I left the house that day, I really was fine with it. I called my mom the next day to show her the house.

Two weeks later, we received a notice from our mortgage company that our interest rate was being lowered, and thus, the house payment meaning we were keeping the house and would not have to move. Now, I'm conversing again with God, and He is showing me clearly that I need to, and MUST, trust Him no matter what happens, no matter where I live, no matter anything. I winked at Him, and said, "I got it!" I thanked HIM, and thanked HIM and thanked HIM.

THE PARK

We have a state park right around the corner from our house with a guard shack at the entrance where a parking attendant sits to take the fee as you enter. I thought, what a perfect, safe, simple, close-to-home job for the girls! The park ranger happened to go to my church, so I called him one day to ask about the position. He said he had people standing in line for that job and had already hired several people for the summer season. I thought, darn, we missed that opportunity.

A few days later, he called and said he had been thinking about my family. The park had a beach putt-putt and concession area the state had been running for years. When they decided they weren't going to run it anymore, he needed to find someone in the private sector to take over the concessions and putt-putt. I laughed out loud, "How in the world did any of that make you think of us?" He answered, "Well, because you have all those kids, and you have the business experience from the spa." Everyone knew we had closed the spa. I assured him that I had no idea how to run a concession stand. I had never even been to that part of the park to see the area. "I really don't think I'm the one for the job." He was obviously under a time crunch because he said, "Why don't you just come down and take a look, and I can share more of the details with you." I thought, "Okay, fine, going to take a look can't hurt." I asked him to let the people at the guard shack know I was coming so I didn't have to pay the $5 fee. I met him at the office and followed him to the beach area. It was beautiful, like going to the beach near my own back yard, yet I never knew it existed. There were picnic tables, grills, gazebos, swings, a playground, a putt-putt course, and a raggedy, beat-up little building they called the concession stand. As soon as he opened the door, I was trying to figure out how I could get a tanning bed and pedicure station inside. We sat outside on top of a picnic table while he explained how the commission structure worked. He told me it would be a great work opportunity for our children. He was right. Every one of our children has worked at "the concession stand," as we refer to it. We redid the whole place and turned it into a tropical paradise, decorating with palm trees to give it a Caribbean feel. We sold anything and everything you could possibly need at the beach from swim suits to beach towels to charcoal and, of course, ice cream and concessions. Every person who walked in the door said, "Wow, I don't remember this place looking like this when I came here as a kid!" or, "This is the nicest concession stand I have ever seen at a state park!" It was a huge success. We still work that concession stand every year from Memorial Day to Labor Day, but now with a different goal.

After a few lavish Christmases, I decided I wanted us to consider something different. I made a motion at our November 2011 family meeting, "I move that no one gets Christmas presents this year and we use the money we would normally spend on each other to take gifts to children living in a Haitian orphanage." If you are familiar with Robert's Rules of Order, you know that when you make a motion, it requires a second motion before you can have any discussion. That did NOT happen. There was no second to the motion, however, there was a lot of discussion, the first of which, "Can you define, 'No one gets any presents?'" The questions continued, and after seven or eight minutes, I reminded everyone that we needed a second to the motion. I got a second, and now it was time for a vote. Slowly, but surely, hands began to go up. It was unanimous, we were going to Haiti. Since it was late November, if we were going for Christmas, we had less than thirty days to find an already planned "mission trip," and get passports, airline tickets, and funding. We wrote a letter to everyone we knew asking for help. I spent days on the internet trying to find a planned mission trip. They just did not exist for Christmas. I started calling and googling anything I could find that could be a possible opportunity. I googled orphanages, Guest Houses, Mission Trips, Haiti; everything was a dead end. Everyone I talked to pretty much laughed at me, "You want to go to Haiti for Christmas? All the missionaries go home for Christmas; there is no one to guide you on a mission trip in Haiti at Christmas." Finally, it hit me, the shoe boxes, Samaritan's Purse, they hand out shoe boxes at Christmas. I thought, "I'll call them and we can distribute their Christmas shoe boxes in Haiti." Call after call sent me to other contacts, "We don't handle Haiti here, you'll need to call France." I called France, "We don't distribute to Haiti through France. You will need to call Canada." Call after call, followed by rejection and bad information. Finally, I spoke with the person in charge of shoe box distribution in Haiti, which was located in England, "Hi, my name is Linda. My family is going to Haiti this Christmas to serve in orphanages and because we will be there on Christmas Day, we would love to hand out the shoe boxes that are going to Haiti." The response followed, "Oh, I'm sorry ma'am. First of all, we don't actually hand out the shoe boxes ON Christmas Day. We distribute our shoe boxes through local pastors in the communities, and they determine when and where to pass out the boxes which are passed out through the year at different events." My heart was crushed. I thought, "This trip is a stupid idea; I can't find anywhere for us to go, or anything for us to do, or anywhere for us to stay." Most of the responses I got were people telling me about their next available mission trip and how they would love to book us for February or May. This was so discouraging; not to mention all the issues we had with our passports - the two children born in Haiti had two different birthdays, each! I had even taken homemade Christmas cookies to the main Passport Office in Atlanta to speed up the process. I was done.

A couple of days later, I couldn't help myself, I started googling again. Right away, I found an orphanage in Haiti with a South Carolina contact number. I called and spoke with Donald Lyons. I told him what I wanted to do, and he said, "You are more than welcome to go and stay at my guest house. I won't be able to lead a mission trip at Christmas, but I will talk with the pastor I work with. I am sure he would be happy to show you around Haiti. I also have an orphanage with seventeen girls who would love for you to join them for Christmas." We went to Haiti, stayed at My Father's Guest House, and spent Christmas with the seventeen girls. We met Pastor Maxeau who did show us around Haiti. We had the time of our lives; indescribable. You would have to see it, smell it, and feel it for yourself.

On our third day in Haiti, while we were riding in the back of a cow truck on our way to an orphanage, Pastor Maxeau needed to make a stop. We pulled up and tapped on the gate, as everyone does in Haiti, and security guards came out to slide it open. We saw chickens and goats wandering around the yard and several tractor trailers without cabs. Pastor Maxeau said a friend of his let him use space in a trailer for storage, and he wanted to pick up gifts to bring to his school for Christmas. He opened the gate on the back of the truck and grabbed teddy bears out of boxes. Then I saw him hand two large boxes to my husband; plain cardboard boxes with "SAMARITAN'S PURSE" stamped on all four sides. When I asked, Pastor Maxeau explained, "This is Franklin Graham's office where Samaritan's Purse works when they come to Haiti. A pastor friend gave me boxes of Samaritan's Purse shoeboxes last year. I saved these two. I never really knew why I saved them because I certainly could have used them last year, but something told me to keep them." I lost my mind, "You have got to be kidding me! Are we going to hand them out?" I cried as I asked Pastor Maxeau to repeat the story so I could make sure I heard him correctly. "You saved these boxes from LAST year?" I asked. "Yes," he said. I told him, "You saved these boxes for me! Before we even knew we were coming to Haiti, God knew. He knew I wanted us to hand out these boxes, so He told you to save them. He knew you were going to be the pastor showing us around Haiti so He kept them here safe and sound waiting for us." I was overcome! There I was calling England, France, and Canada, losing my mind because I couldn't coordinate what I wanted how I wanted it! We left and drove to Gallet Chambon to hand out our gifts plus what Pastor Maxeau saved. When we arrived at the school, it was unbelievable. There were children everywhere. What I hoped would be a joyful experience handing out boxes ended sadly because there was not enough. We had to take the boxes and the candy apart to give only one item to each child. I'll never forget the last child, a boy, who walked up for a gift. David said, "All we have left is a hot pink toy cell phone. We can't give him that." But, we did. The look in that little boy's eyes was the same as if we had handed him a million dollars. He was so thankful.

On Christmas Day 2011, Pastor Maxeau took us to LifeSaver Orphanage. We got out of the cow truck sweating in the hot Haiti sun, and stumbled past a pile of trash with a goat on one side, a pig on the other, and two little boys on either end, all rifling through the heap, looking for food. We walked past raw sewage running down the street and stepped up makeshift broken concrete steps to enter the orphanage. We continued up several flights of stairs. As the stench grew stronger, I turned around and told the girls, no matter what, not to laugh or say anything inappropriate about the odor. We learned later, the floors we walked up were actually the levels where they had school. We got to the living quarters. I remember the horrible smell, aquamarine walls, a big table in the kitchen area, and the children. We didn't have much with us, but pulled out the crafts and coloring books to start playing at the table. Then, we watched a miracle happen. We opened the suitcase and pulled out gifts. There were twenty-seven children, and somehow, we had a gift and pair of flip flops for each child. It was like the suitcase was manufacturing gifts and shoes. When we were finished, Pastor Maxeau said the children wanted to thank us by singing for us. And, sing they did, for at least thirty minutes. It was hot, the place stunk, but the singing was amazing! My favorite song was *This Little Light of Mine*. They sang in English, Spanish, and Creole.

Before we left, we sat down to speak with the parents who ran the orphanage, who had four children of their own. We learned the father, Pastor Paul, was a music teacher at the school. Many of the children had been his students, and after the earthquake, they had no place to go. The stability of the school, the place where they came for music lessons, caused the children to turn to Pastor Paul's home. One by one, he took in the children, and before he knew it, had twenty-seven plus his four. We were overwhelmed by the story and wanted to help. We asked Pastor Paul his greatest need. He looked at us with tears in his eyes, and responded, "You have already met our greatest need." David and I stared at each other as we waited for Pastor Maxeau to translate. We couldn't imagine what he was talking about. All we had shared was a few crayons, some coloring books, a couple of Barbie dolls, some flip flops, and a few matchbox cars. Then Pastor Maxeau spoke, "You have provided his children with shoes. That is their greatest need and what they have been praying for. You provided them with an answer to their prayers, and they are very grateful." We wanted to help more. We gave $400 toward buying a generator. Our hearts were broken, yet full, when we left that day. All I could think was how amazing those kids sang. It blew my mind. Even though their circumstances were horrible, they were singing about the joy of Jesus. I thought, they need to come to the United States and show children that when Jesus is all you have, you realize He is all you need.

Every day when we returned to the guest house there would be two or three little boys waiting outside the gate. The guest house provided a delicious breakfast and dinner for us, however, because we would be out during the day, we were told to bring snacks and food for lunch. Before we left, I had accumulated pop tarts, crackers, and Slim Jims; the exact amount we would need for lunch and two snacks every day. Well, each day when we got back to the guest house, one of us would sneak back out to give peanut butter crackers to these little boys. We would also sneak extra crackers into our bags when we left for the day so we could throw them from the truck to the children on the street. One afternoon, David saw us taking the crackers out to give the boys at the gate. He told us not to because we were going to run out of food before the end of the week. He also said the Guest House manager didn't want us to feed anyone at the gate because it could cause problems. The next day, he noticed we were throwing peanut butter crackers from the back of the cow truck. Again he told us, "We only have a certain number of snacks. You can't keep throwing them out because we will be out of food before we leave." Those crackers multiplied like fish and loaves. We watched it happen every day; it was unbelievable. When we got home, we had packages of peanut butter crackers left in our suitcases.

Once home, at our February family meeting, I asked everyone if our Christmas trip was a one-time thing, or if they wanted to go again. I can still hear Jasmine's response, "Mrs. Linda, we have to go back. Those kids are counting on us." We have been back every year since 2011.

On our 2012 trip, we went back to LifeSaver Orphanage on Christmas Day. They had a party for us and a sign welcoming our family. They sang for us, and it was even better than the last year. On our way back to the guest house that night, I told Pastor Maxeau my thoughts from the year before, and said, "I think those kids need to come to the United States to sing as a choir." He looked back at me and said with his heavy Haitian accent, "Oh, Mama Linda, everyone thinks that. Every American I bring here to hear them sing says the same thing, but no one has ever done anything about it. It is also Pastor Paul and the children's dream to come to America and sing as a choir." Was I really hearing what he was saying? Now, I was determined.

By 2013, we were helping Pastor Maxeau pay his teachers' salaries at Gallet Chambon School. We worked hard all year long to raise funds to give him at Christmas for whatever projects needed it. We brought Christmas presents and school supplies for more and more children each year. It was funny; it took those two years working together for us to trust him, and it took him that long to trust us. He has told us many times since that he would often exchange information with mission team members, but they didn't contact him. He said, "But you, you just keep coming back."

FRIENDS

In 2011, my friend Diane called me to say she wasn't feeling well. When I finally got to the bottom of it, she was more than not feeling well. She had been buckled over on the bathroom floor for nights in gut-wrenching pain. After several trips to many doctors, we got the diagnosis of Stage IV colon cancer.

I remember sitting in the waiting room at Emory with her husband, waiting for the doctor after one of her surgeries. He called Chad into one of those little side rooms. I didn't wait to be asked to join them, I just went in. On a dry erase board, the doctor drew Diane's colon on the board and explained what he had done. He also explained that he couldn't do anymore. I couldn't break down because I was watching Chad fall to pieces. I made a commitment that day to see Diane through the road ahead, and I did. We went to every doctor appointment, cancer seminar, and chemotherapy treatment together. We lived at the hospital for days at a time. We were the happiest people at every chemotherapy session. We laughed and cried and laughed and cried. We dressed up like movie stars for the hospital visits. We had the sassiest coolers with the best snacks to take to chemo. We even bought extra sassy coolers to give away to other cancer patients. We always had the best food. Chad would pack us organic blueberries, organic humus, organic granola bars, and organic vegetables. I'm pretty sure he even packed organic paper towels and napkins. We would stop on our way home from chemo at TGIFridays and have big juicy hamburgers with icy Cokes, but never told him. I remember one time, we were sitting in the bar area at a booth at TGIFridays near the Mall of Georgia during an off time of the day. We were the only ones there and close enough to the bartender that she could have a conversation with us. We were laughing and just having a blast. When the bartender was delivering our food, she noticed that Diane had a tube running out of her shirt. It was the chemo bag that she had to wear home for three days after we left each treatment. She stared at the tube, then stared at us, and asked, "Is everything ok?" I'd always answer for Diane, "Nope, she has Stage IV colon cancer. She's taking chemo right now. Things are really bad. How are things with you?" We had so many opportunities to share about Jesus, all because of our joy in the midst of our circumstances. Only

Jesus could provide what we had during that season.
No one ever thought Diane was sick; she looked great. Now, they didn't see what I saw. She threw up constantly. I had green throw up bags with me at all times; in my purse, in my car, at my house, everywhere. But, we kept on going. We struggled through. I made her put on makeup and dress up to go shopping, out to eat, and to have fun.
On Valentine's Day, a big group of friends from our Sunday school class got together to go to a Valentine's Dance held in a high school gym where they had dinner, door prizes, and a deejay. It was a blast! Diane and Chad looked amazing. She loved to dance, and so did I. Most of the evening, it was the two of us on the dance floor. My husband will never forgive me if I don't tell you that he won Best Male Dancer of the evening. He had the women screaming and yelling to vote for him! I have some fabulous pictures of Chad and Diane slow dancing. She looked amazing. We shopped for days for that dress. It was Diane's last great night out.

She passed away at 9:20 AM on April 22, 2012. Chad and I were on either side of the hospital bed set up in her living room by Hospice. We were each holding one of her hands, and her sons were there. She had had a horrible week; she was so young and otherwise healthy, and her heart just wouldn't stop beating. Chad called me Sunday and said, "You need to come and say, 'Good Bye.' She hasn't moved all day. I don't think she will make it through the night." I rushed over to her house. When I got there, she sat straight up in the bed, and said, "Hello." I looked at Chad, and he just shook his head as if to say, "Really?" I asked Chad to get her something to eat, mostly to give him a break. I jumped into the hospital bed with her, as I always did, and when Chad left, she leaned over, and said, "I want to tell you a secret." Then she whispered to me, "Linda, I want you to know, I'm dying." I looked back at her and said, "I know you are." She continued, "I'm leaving to go to heaven soon, and I'm going to miss you. I love you." I reminded her that I would be there with her in less than fifteen minutes. On one of our long eight hour chemo days, we had discussed, among many other things, God's timing. We figured out mathematically that if a day to the Lord is like 1000 years to us, then by the time Diane would get inside the gates of heaven and receive directions to her mansion, I would be there. We figured it would only seem like fifteen minutes according to heaven's time.

When Chad returned with the food, she was already asleep. That was the last conversation we had. She left us on that Thursday. Her favorite number was 1111. She died at 9:20, but the time stuck on the coffee maker in her kitchen was 11:11. I seemed to see that number everywhere for a while. We set our orphan sponsorship amount at $11.11 in honor of Diane.

DIMITRY

My friend Macarena got very sick. After several tests, the doctor said she would need to have a simple operation so everything would be back to normal. "It will be quick, in and out of the hospital, all in one day." That didn't happen. Things went wrong.

When I received the call from Macarena's husband that she would not be coming home from the hospital that night because of some complications, I rushed back. When I walked into her room and saw her distraught, sickly face, I lost it. I had to go out in the hallway where I called out directly to God, "Seriously? I mean really? This is enough, first Myrna, then Diane, and now Macarena? I can't do this again. I don't want to do this again. I'm not doing this again." I called another friend while sitting by the elevator in the hospital, had an ugly cry for about five minutes, then hung up, got myself together, and walked back into the room with Macarena. I stayed until they released her.

What started as an "in and out" one-day surgery left her on her back for two weeks. During this time, she read the Bible, watched videos and movies, and kept updated with friends on Facebook. One day, while she was scrolling through, she saw a picture of a blond teenager on Kathy's Facebook page. Kathy, the Michigan lady who came to the spa to do the makeup class, had gone to Ukraine and adopted a teenage boy. He had grown up in the orphanage with three others who, having been raised together, were a tight-knit group. When Kathy finalized her adoption and returned to the United States with her new son, she left behind this last boy who had not been adopted. Macarena was mesmerized by the picture, and felt she needed to jump out of bed and go to Ukraine to get this young man. She knew her husband would be the biggest obstacle. She had been working on him for the last year or so to become a foster parent. She wanted to attend the foster care parenting classes to start the process but he was dead set against it. She told God (and me) the only way for her to even bring up the young Ukrainian boy would be for God to prepare Troy's heart, so she prayed. I prayed. She waited for weeks to bring it up. Then one day, they were both on separate computers looking at stuff, and she just leaned over, and said, "Have you seen this?" She showed him the picture of the boy still in the orphanage in Ukraine. Troy looked at the picture, and said, "He looks just like me." He took Macarena's iPad to read the story. "We need to do something. What do we have to do to bring him here?" And so, the "Bringing Dima Home" campaign began.

After many months of raising funds, social worker visits, home studies, and much more, Macarena and Troy traveled to Ukraine in the middle of one of the worst times in its history. Planes were being shot down, armored tanks were everywhere, and government agencies were under threat, if not occupation. They walked into the Ukrainian courthouse to sign some final paperwork while the Ukrainian flag flew, and when they walked out two hours later, the Russian flag was overhead.

The final step in bringing Dima home was the passport. However, because of all the turmoil, the government buildings had been closed. Macarena and Troy were there for weeks. Macarena was scared. She skyped daily while waiting, and waiting, and waiting. She told me she wanted me to be prepared to take in, care for, and raise her children if she didn't return, to which I responded, "Oh, you are going to return, girlfriend. God is not giving me three more children." There was no answer to getting the final step completed. No one knew when the government buildings would reopen. Ukraine felt if they sent government workers in to work, Russia would blow up those buildings. Macarena struggled with leaving her husband behind in Ukraine with Dima to come home to be with her three children here. She contacted me weeping. We prayed, we cried, we prayed hard, we cried more, and prayed harder. We both knew the only way for this to be resolved and finalized was for God to intervene. She skyped the next morning saying they had received a phone call from their Ukrainian facilitator. The passport was ready and they were coming home. I said, "Oh, so everything is better there now, the courthouse and government buildings have reopened?" She said, "No, it's Saturday here, there is nothing open. When I asked the facilitator how we got the passport, he said he had no explanation for where or how we got this passport." God is such a show off, isn't He?

UGANDAN THUNDER AND MELINDA

On our Christmas 2014 trip to Haiti, we again went to the LifeSaver Orphanage. After they finished singing for us, I stood up and told them we wanted to bring them to the United States as a choir. The delay in speaking through an interpreter is nerve wracking. As I watched Pastor Maxeau translate, their faces lit up, and they clapped and screamed and yelled with excitement. I told them the only way any of it would begin to be possible was through them. I said they, as orphans, had a special place in God's heart, and their prayers would be answered. I explained what a huge project this was, how we needed their prayers for a bus, a place to stay, for visas, passports, places to sing, the entire project. We prayed that night, and asked them to keep on praying.

I had heard about Ugandan Thunder, an African choir who performed several times in churches close to our home, but we never were able to see them. When we returned in 2015, and I started to wrap my mind around the Haitian choir coming to America, I remembered the choir from Africa. I ran into Megan who was now a middle school coach, and shared my dream with her. She said, "You know, my college roommate interned with Ugandan Thunder. Yeah, she was on the road with them every day for eight months, or so." A week later, I was at Bar H BBQ with Macarena, Megan's college roommate, and a yellow legal pad filled with questions. By the end of the meal, it was decided that I needed to meet with Melinda who was the road manager of Ugandan Thunder, and had been there from the beginning. Megan's roommate assured me she would be more than happy to set me on the right track. I was given all of Melinda's contact information and then another wait began. It took months to get any response. Then one day, I was at our local Walmart when I came out and saw the Ugandan Thunder van. I flipped out, "Oh, my goodness, they are here." I googled their calendar, and sure enough, they were going to be at a church thirty minutes from my house that night. I had still never seen them, but I also wanted to talk to Melinda. I thought, "She has to be inside Walmart. How weird is it going to be if I go to Customer Service and have them page her to the front of the store? Okay, maybe too weird, so I will just stay here and stalk the van until she comes out." In the meantime, I wrote a note on a card and put it on the window of the van. I messaged Melinda to tell her I was sitting in the Toccoa Walmart parking lot staking out her van. I didn't hear anything so left my note asking whoever got it to have Melinda call me. I went to hear the performance that night. I was blown away. I knew more than ever the kids from the LifeSaver orphanage could do this. I waited afterward to meet Melinda only to learn she wasn't there. Finally, almost six months after meeting Megan's roommate, I got a lunch appointment with Melinda at the Zaxby's in Madison,

Georgia. Macarena went with me. I spent three days writing down all the questions I had. "What happens if someone gets hurt?" "Do you get insurance for everyone?" "How do you feed them?" "How can you afford gas?" "Where did you get those amazing vans?" The night before the scheduled meeting, I asked David if he had anything specific he thought I should ask her. He said, "Yes. Ask her how they do what they do."

It was near Melinda's birthday, and Macarena and I brought her a gift. Her husband was with her. I started off with my questions. She had a great big white notebook; actually, I think she had two. She was showing me the forms and paperwork, and explained how her organization was feeding over 5000 orphans. She showed me they were in the process of building a medical facility in Uganda. She was showing me all the P3 and P4 forms that had to be filled out and telling me Homeland Security would be involved concerning where the children could stay. She asked me about passports, and visas, and all sorts of things that I had absolutely no idea about. My eyeballs started poking out of my head in confusion. Then, about an hour and fifteen minutes into our discussion, she looked across the table at me and said, "Would you like me to come and help you?" I looked up, and she repeated her question. I replied, "I don't understand what you mean by help me?" "Would you like me to leave Ugandan Thunder to help you do in Haiti what we have accomplished in Uganda?" At that moment, something happened that has only happened four or five times in my life. I was speechless. I didn't even know what to say if I wasn't speechless because I couldn't speak, or maybe that is speechlessness. We left that day agreeing she and her husband would pray, and Macarena and I would discuss the whole idea with our husbands; then we would meet again in a couple of weeks.

To make a long story short, Melinda Fowler, formerly of Ugandan Thunder, began working with Love Him Love Them, on September 21, 2015, as our first and only employee. She will be our road manager and tour director. When she told Ugandan Thunder she was leaving, and why, they asked if they could do a benefit concert for us. That blew my mind. We organized a concert and Ugandan Thunder sang to raise funds for our choir on October 23, 2015. We had an all-day benefit starting at the Barnes Academy Christian School who hosted a catered lunch for the choir. Ugandan Thunder sang for the school and parents, then went to Anderson and sang at the Anderson Mall. Chick-fil-a fed the choir supper, and we headed to The Carpenter's Church where we had the most amazing spirit-filled, fun evening ever. The pastor, Kendall Hicks, was so supportive, it was amazing. You would have thought we had written a script for him to get up and challenge the audience that night to support us. It was crazy for me to grasp that orphans from Uganda were singing to raise funds for orphans from Haiti who would then be coming to America to sing to raise funds for orphans in Ukraine and Haiti. What an international experience!

CONNECTIONS

Sarah LeCroy is the founder of Barnes Academy in Hartwell, Georgia; a Christian school open to all students and families, pre-K to 12th grade. I contacted her to ask if I could share the story about the choir coming to the U.S. She was more than excited and invited me to share at Barnes Academy's weekly Friday chapel. I was overwhelmed. I'll never forget the first time she introduced me to her students and staff, "This is my friend, CRAZY LINDA!!" And, that is exactly what every child and staff member have called me since that day, even the principal. Chapel at that school was amazing. I wanted to go back every Friday and did for several weeks. I was in awe of the Holy Spirit's presence there with the students. The worship time was beautiful, the speakers incredible. Once Sarah heard our story, she was all in. The school sponsored every child in the choir with our $11.11 monthly child sponsorship program. She offered her entire school for the choir to use as a home base, the vans, school bus, and the chapel. She is the reason we were able to connect with Kendall Hicks at The Carpenter's Church for our benefit concert. She wanted the Ugandan Thunder Choir to come to Barnes Academy that day, and as I shared earlier, Sarah and the school provided a catered lunch as well as an audience. She invited the student's parents, friends, and others to the performance, which led to introductions to several pastors and churches, which led to contacts with more pastors and churches. This was the spark we needed, and we are so grateful for all they have done.

ONGOING

When I began writing this in February, we had less than four months before the choir would set foot on American soil to sing. In that time period, costumes have been sewn and fitted, funds for flights have been raised, Melinda and I just submitted the final request for further evidence in the Homeland Security packet, and we have an appointment with the Haitian Embassy June 7th with the kids for the final procurement of their visas.

Doug Vermilya, 2016 Teacher of the Year for North Habersham Middle School, who is a part of our weekly Bible study introduced us to Heather Hawkins, a fellow NHMS teacher, who had a desire to pray specifically for people in cars she passed on her commute, so shared with us the concept of "Prayer Petals." Just so happens, Kelly Breymeir of Capri Deigns is also a member of our weekly Bible study, and with many others working together, we developed a magnetized product with removable petals that allow you to pray together as a family, group, or church for specific needs such as Relationships, Health, Leadership, Salvation, and Finances. You can go to **www.P41A.com** to learn all about how to P-ray 4 1 A-nother!

We have a committee working on a HUGE golf tournament for next year to help raise funds. They are involving Atlanta Falcons players, UGA golf players, and much, much more; more than I could have ever hoped for or even imagined. The choir is completely booked from June 28th thru October 3rd with only a few week days available.

My prayer is that I can look back once this book is complete and just laugh. I'm not laughing right now but I should be because I know God is smiling. He puts everything together as He wants to meet the needs of His people and to change the hearts of his people to glorify Him. All I need to do is continue to make HIS desires mine. God continues to show His faithfulness. Every time my phone rings and a strange number shows up, I put on my spiritual seatbelt, and think, "Hang on, Linda, here we go!"

How what everyone said could NEVER happen HAPPENNED

I am on the plane in Haiti headed back to the United States as I am typing this on my iPad. The sole purpose for this quick trip to Haiti was to escort the 30 individuals we have been planning for years now to bring to the United States as a choir. Our appointment at the US Embassy in Haiti was Tuesday, June 7th (another 7) at 9:30 am. Pastor Maxeau drove me to the orphanage and all the children were dressed in their Sunday best with a Purple Love HIM Love Them T-shirts over top. As soon as I walked in the Life Saver orphanage the children began singing "Faithful". I love that song and didn't even know it was in their repertoire. We loaded up the 15 passenger van, Pastor Maxeau's truck and a tap-tap we rented for the day. The drive to the embassy was surreal for me. I was sitting in the same seat in Pastor Maxeau's truck that we had the original conversation of the vision to bring the choir. Half of the planning and all of the conversations were done in this truck riding on the rocky roads of Haiti.

When we arrived the line outside the embassy looked like one for a new ride at Six Flags. People were everywhere. As we unloaded our

3 vehicles and headed to find our place in the line EVERYONE gave us that same look you give a lady walking on a plane with 3 screaming babies. None wanted all of us in front of them in the line. I immediately started taking pictures and a LOUD foghorn went off and 2 guards came up to stop me yelling "NO PHOTO'S Madame". They took my phone and told me I could have it upon exiting the embassy. And then the waiting began. We waited outside in 105 degree Haitian heat. We went through the first line and then got inside, well sort of inside, then we waited in another outside area, this time there were benches though! I kept asking all the guards, "If this is really the American embassy, "Where is the air-conditioning? And more importantly where is the Diet Coke?" They had neither. Once we were inside...you guessed it, we were in another line. When we were finally called up to the window we were told we owed an additional $30 per person per visa. "OK, I thought and started calculating in my head, because they took my phone outside I had no calculator", Then she said "it can only be paid in cash". Right when she said "Cash" I had calculated $900. Pastor Paul from the orphanage was beside me. He just looked at me.
The Carpenter's Church in Anderson had donated the final $1000.00 for the water filtration system in Haiti and I brought that money with me to Haiti to give to Pastor Maxeau. When I arrived in Haiti I tried to give it to him and he said, "No, just wait, I will get it before you leave". Because of that I had the cash in my purse so I took the $1000.00 and paid the US Embassy cashier. Then, we moved to ....another line. After a very long time and with children who were laying on top of each other on the few chairs provided they asked us to pair up in groups of 1 adult and 3 children and have all of our paperwork ready. They called the first group. It was Pastor Paul, Gertie, Eldo and Belinda. I went with them to the window. The gentleman behind the glass window asked for the paperwork speaking thru his microphone headset. He asked Eldo (in Creole) Where are your parents? Why are you in the orphanage? Do you know this lady? (Pointing to me) Eldo responded; he didn't know where his parents were. The last time he saw them was in City Solei (the poorest of the poorest cities in Haiti) over 9 years ago. And Yes, He knew Mama Linda. He asked Pastor Paul (the father of the orphanage) nothing.

And then the "Examination" (as Pastor Paul continued to refer to it throughout the next hour) began. The US embassy worker whose name was David started with the interrogation "How long has your organization been in existence?"
"Since 1998". "Where did the idea come from to bring this choir to the United States?"
"My family came in December 2011 and these children sang for us. When we left that day we said "These children need to come to America to show the children in the United States that when Jesus is all you have you realize that Jesus is all you need." We have been working and raising funds since that time"
Then David (US embassy David) asked me "How do you plan to transport these children and where will they be staying?" I pulled out the amazing book that Melinda Fowler had put together with all of our information and showed them a picture of the Barnes Academy school bus and the house at Barnes. We slid the notebook under the small opening at the bottom of the window counter. Then David took off his headset and disappeared with the book and we waited.
When he returned he said he noticed in the book there was a tour schedule and wanted to know where the children would be staying when we were traveling. I explained how each church would be providing host homes.
"Have you ever brought a child from Haiti to the United States before?" (I couldn't figure out what his angle was with this question, and my mind was racing. Would it be good or bad that I had or had not brought children before? If he wants me to say YES, I could say YES because I was a part of bringing my children from Haiti, but if he wants me to say "NO", I could say "No" because I haven't really brought any children from Haiti.

I forgot to tell you about earlier in the morning before we arrived at the Embassy while we were at the orphanage. After the children sang "Faithful" Pastor Maxeau prayed and also explained to the children that we had all done everything we could do. All the paperwork was filed and there was nothing any of us could do now; only God could make anything move forward. He explained to the children some possible questions he thought they may get asked. But his final statement was "No matter, what they ask you, be sure to tell the truth."

So, with that ringing in my ear I answered "No, I have never brought children from Haiti to the United States before"
"Our concern here at the United States Embassy, Mrs. Gunter is that these children are all orphans and that you may have some sort of an adoption process and plan for these children. We need you to convince us this is not what is happening."
I said "Ok...um....well...., we do not discuss adoptions during any of our presentations. I could provide you with the plane tickets, that will show a return date to prove they are returning, (when I get them, but I don't have them yet because we need the visas first) I can show you the tour schedule that finishes on October 2nd" He interrupted me and said "I don't want to see any of that, I want YOU to convince ME that these children are coming back to Haiti" I looked straight back at him through the glass window and said emphatically "Oh, you better believe they are coming back, I can guarantee you that, they are all coming back!" He said "Thank you" and left the window.
About 5 minutes later he returned with another man and said, "Please bring me each child's passport and paperwork". I asked "Do you need to see each child?" "No, no, just the papers please." And so the paper gathering of 30 people began, we returned to the window and placed them all under the glass.
He said "OK, we will do a name search on each child and you can pick up your visas and passports at the DHL office in one week." "So, they are all approved?" I asked. "Yes, Yes" they assured me. "And I can go ahead and book their plane tickets?"
"We can't tell you to book your tickets" I interrupted them and asked "If it were you would YOU book the plane tickets?"
They both responded "They are all children, there is no reason any problems would arise with a name check, I would go ahead and book their flights, especially if it will save you money on the flight by not waiting the extra week until you have the visas in your hands".

And with that, I went to explain to the children we were all approved. They danced and sang and screamed and we got in trouble and the guards told us to be quiet. Actually they said very sternly "SILENCE!" So we went outside and danced and celebrated and screamed and jumped for joy. And as any great event in life should be celebrated with children we went out for cake and pizza.

It is a strange feeling when God accomplishes something that others tell you is completely impossible and will never happen. It is an unbelievable feeling when it happens in a strange way. They never asked the kids to sing. They didn't even talk with, acknowledge or look at each child. They never questioned our interpreter about his plans or family or anything. They didn't ask about the fact that an entire family and an entire orphanage was coming to the states. I don't think I will ever forget the statement "I just need YOU to convince ME they are coming back."
Reminds me of someone else who WE all need to be convinced IS coming back!

Linda and her Dad both graduating from college...just a few years apart

Linda's Mom and sisters Karen and Beth

David's Family L-R Robert, Lynn, Linda, David, John Henry, Susie, Linda, John, Melissa, Tracy and Matt. The GUNTER'S

Linda and David at the 2015 Barnes Academy Prom

One of the 2 family photos we have
with all the kids 2007 (only people with LARGE families will understand
how it is possible to only have 2 photo's with EVERYONE)
L-R (back row) Jeanna, Raphael, Stacha, Kendra
L-R (front row) Aleena, Jazzy, David, Linda

Chad and Diane at Valentine Dinner 2012

Linda and Diane Christmas 2011. She REALLY wanted to go to Haiti with us!

The 3 girls we still have at home Aleena (18), Jazzy (16) and Jeanna (19)

Jeanna, Linda, Jazzy, Aleena 2015

L-R Aleena, Raphael, Stacha, Jeanna, Jazzy Linda & David

Girls shopping Jazzy, Aleena, Linda, Jeanna and Georgia

Fun with Georgia
L-R Jazzy, David, Georgia, Jeanna, Linda and Aleena

Father's Day 2014 at Tugaloo State Park Concession Stand
L-R Georgia, Linda, Jeanna, David, Jazzy and Aleena

Macarena and DImitry Skyping Linda and Jazmine from Ukraine

Macarena arriving in the United States from Ukraine with Dimitry

A few of our Love HIM Love them volunteers who meet weekly at our home for Bible Study

Raising funds for LHLT at a festival
L-R Aleena, Dalesha, Cameron, Dima, Macarena, Troy, Jazzy & Jeanna

Teachers from Valley of Hope Gallet Chambon School in Haiti and Mission Trip participants 2014

Tashay, Brianna, Jelaya, Dalesha Keke Jazzy and Caraiah packing shoes for Haiti

Volunteers serving plates at Annual Thanksgiving Meal we deliver to Homeless and Homebound
L-R Vergil, Amy, Carrie, Martha, Barbara (Troy's mom) and Barbara (my mom) 2015

Marissa and Carrie helping at Thanksgiving

Pastor Maxeau and David (2 peas in a pod)

Linda and ANN, Pastor Maxeau's wife in Haiti at St. Therese's wedding

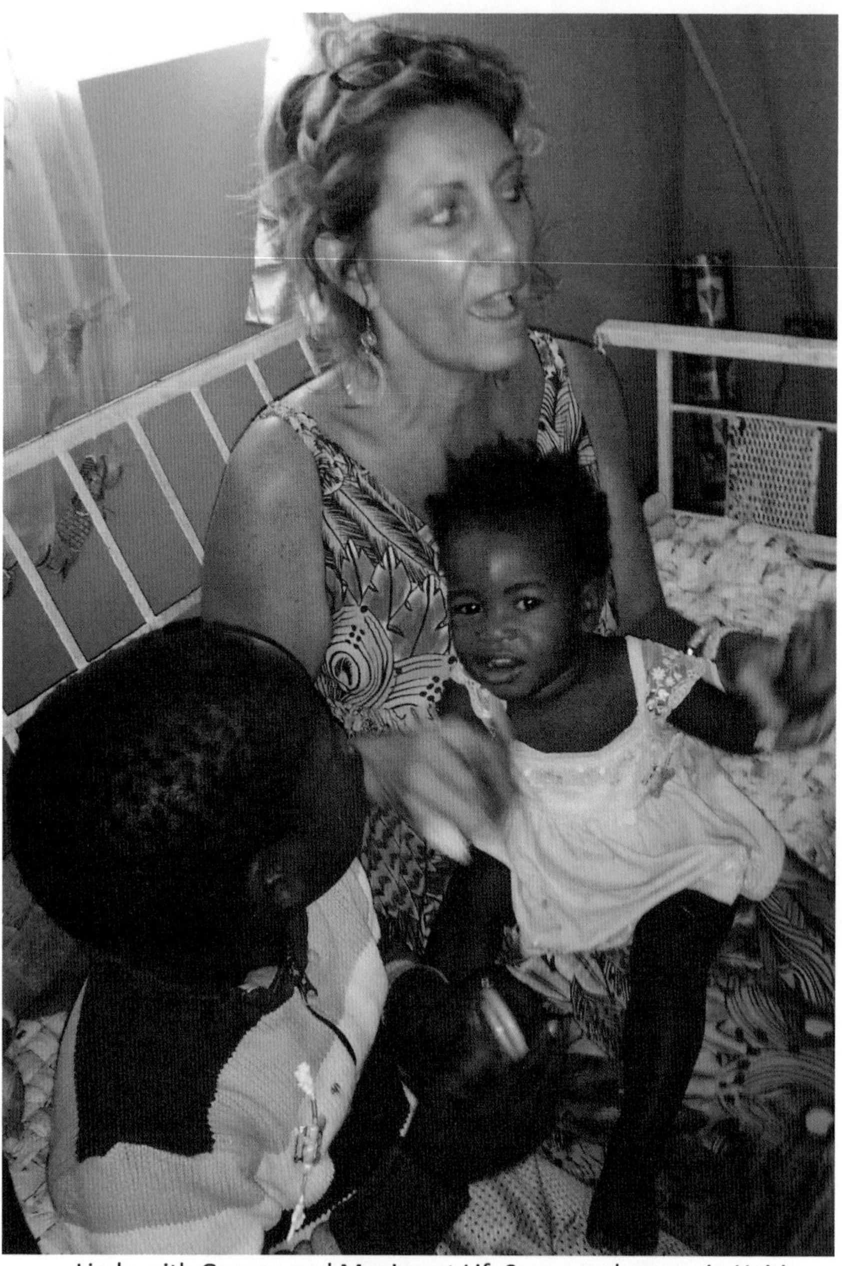

Linda with Gerson and Magine at LifeSaver orphanage in Haiti Christmas Day 2011. First time we heard the children sing.

Linda celebrating her birthday with The Hope and Love orphanage & Naomi

Our 2nd Christmas with the 17 girls from the HUG orphanage. We went to the beach. (2012)

Christmas 2015 returning from Haiti at the Atlanta Airport
L-R Jazzy, David, Aleena, Linda, Chase, Charlene, Lauren, Jeanna, Anthony and Luke

Volunteers for Special Needs Adult Valentine Dance 2014
L-R Linda, Tanya, Nora, Kelly, Macarena and Torey

Jeanna, Aleena and Jazzy on top of Pastor Maxeau's house in Haiti

July 4th 2015 Special Needs Adult Annual Summer BBQ and Putt Putt Competition with Watermelon Seed Spitting

Linda, ST. Therese (mother of HUG orphanage) and Macarena in Haiti

Linda with St. Therese, (mother of the HUG orphanage, the very first orphanage the Gunter's visited in Haiti in 2011) as her maid of honor in 2014. They share the same birthday too.

FAMILIES Working TOGETHER

Melinda Fowler

Pastor Maxeau and Linda presenting a goat for the entrepreneurial program in Haiti

Weekly Bible Study group at The Gunter's Praying over Choir Project

Preparing to speak at North Habersham Middle School
The combined 8th grade classes sponsor every child in the choir for $11.11 monthly and they prepared Christmas Bags to take and also books for our library in Haiti.

Doug and Heather with Prayer Petals

Macarena and Sarah LeCroy of Barnes Academy with Invitation for new After School Program UNDER CONSTRUCTION

Linda and Sarah LeCroy with sponsorships for choir from Barnes Academy

Linda and Macarena

Youngest volunteers Nora and Erin with Amy

Love HIM Love Them
ORPHAN CHOIR FROM HAITI
Performing at
Date:
Starting at
Love Him Love Them
CONTACT MELINDA @ 770-584-5992

Linda and Mirlanda from Lifesaver 2015

2016 Love HIM Love Them Haitian orphan Choir

THE FLIP FLOPS we gave to LifeSaver Choir in 2011
Gertie (lead female vocalist) from the choir

THE Samaritan's Purse box I saw the first year we went to Haiti in 2011

Phyllis (Hostess with the mostest) from the HUG Guest House

P41A bracelets we hand out at our concerts

Standing in line outside the US EMBASSY in Haiti
June 7th 2016
For Visa approval for 30!

This is the picture I took that got my phone taken away at the Embassy.

Walking into the US Embassy in Haiti June 7, 2016 for Visa approval for 30 people.

Made in the USA
Charleston, SC
22 September 2016